F 2 F

Janet Holmes

University of Notre Dame Press

Notre Dame, Indiana

Library of Congress Cataloging-in-Publication Data

Holmes, Janet (Janet A.)
f2f / Janet Holmes.
p.   cm.
Poems.
ISBN-13: 978-0-268-03076-6 (pbk. : alk. paper)
ISBN-10: 0-268-03076-6 (pbk. : alk. paper)
I. Title.
PS3558.O35935F3   2006
811'.54—dc22

2006024197

∞ *The paper in this book meets the guidelines for permanence and durability*
of the Committee on Production Guidelines for Book Longevity of the Council
on Library Resources.

For Al

Contents

Acknowledgments

"Lost on us," "Encounter," "Watches him," "At the worst of it," "Lake," "Elected element," and "Cons/dole" first appeared in *Pleiades*.

"Dark Bar" appeared in *Mid-American Review* in slightly different form.

Personal thanks to Al Greenberg, Kath Jesme, Catherine Daly, Kerri Webster, Martin Corless-Smith, and Cathy Wagner.

Writely

I won't ever know.

You could shape words with your mouth as you read silently.

Whisper them, sibilant, into a translucent ear.

Couldn't catch you doing it.

. . .

Doing it. Yes?

The *O*s like kisses, the smiling *E*s—

You couldn't watch me scratch
with the fountain pen:

~~Read me.~~   Scratching it out.

. . .

The contract mandates camouflage

(you won't watch)

(so I don't care where you begin)

. . .

Can't picture me, can you? We can't picture ourselves.
Not in our "real lives."

Start at the bottom of the page and read up I wouldn't know it.

From: Date: To: Subject:

One day she was there speaking from the flatscreen.
He was there one day saying things.
Typing.
We say *saying,* meaning *writing.*
You liked the things written that were as if said.
She or he "interesting" you.
You stayed online.
[Idiom for *connected.*]
Giving your madeup name.
To himher, whobeit.
You did not, on this level, trust.
You had things to say, meaning *write.*
To the one who died, whom you can't shake.
To the succubus. She stole your manhood.
To one your memory renders foreign.
To the incubus who fucked you unseen & left you a demon baby.
To your mistakes.
To the bodiless Deity.
To your longing.
You say these things, meaning write them, & look at them & click where it says

send.

Reader, you did these things.

Glassicaglia

for now

so long for now!
(wave)
(for now!)   for nowt

        for nought we see   for night   *night-night!*

we see / we see through
it's glass

we   see you through

                see through you now
                                (for now)   (or nigh)
        see

mirror   *error* . . .

for now we see nought through the glass
naught   naughty
nighty night

     dar   kly   kling

     darkling we listen   darkly we see

     through a glass dark   glassy dark
     we they do see through a
     glass darkly

but

mirror   hear
                                    error
it's glass

face to face   f2f   then

they   (for they shall see God)
for now we are seen through a glass darkly

                              error

face to face
can you see   now?

see
              darkly

Comes in at the eyes

(they were little girls)

they and Eurydice
spied on Psyche

(E standing suspicious
        considering   nearly visible
                                       riskous girl)

their moms had said
P was the *most*
beautiful, in such a way

                             to convey
the value of being that

but an impression—
as a direction
            an order
                        and they could see their moms trying
                        to be like P
ah   Desire

. . .

grown women looked frightening
to them

~~even~~ the beautiful ones
especially

all the moms wanted
beautiful daughters, girls
gods would fall for

good, groomed, gifted

who didn't skip a day of cotillion

knew to say no to

E: *no.*

wore   red   all the time
dyed her hair   red
grew long nails   wore omigod comical makeup
                            like a raccoon

smoked

. . .

red red red
nothing like P

moms got migraines

from
looking—

List

Saying *writing*
You are the only one I can talk to

Hearing *reading*
And you are the only one I can talk to

You are not giggling under the tablecloth you are two adults sitting
at expensive computers touch-typing (oh! yes) resting your index
fingers on the F and the J waiting for the incoming ping of the
instanter message like a starting gun

      gd 2 c u again
      wass^?

your form is never more than an extension of such content

no one sees you

and no one sees you

doing it

Lost on us

a goddess's *gotcha:*

Echo a wicked nymph,
gossipy
            and fleet

        (everywhere where)
                        (nowhere)

miss mischief, miss misdirection, miss—

(*over here*—)

girl with no door on her mouth
. . .

gotcha: a wordless curse
and pretty soon

E's skeleton rises through her body

      it takes days

the flesh sinking away (sinking in?)
(rinsed muslin, drapery)

tibia so thin she circles it with one finger

    ribcage

    pelvis

her bones briefly illumine,
neonish,
from within

then, fog   then, suggestion.
. . .

hands wave through her
self
no resistance
where the torso
was

no hands
ex-hands

(am I invisible?)

                                            (am

I?)

. . .

(did I do this to myself?)

. . .

thinks

this is the curse

(it isn't)

GODDESS: LISTEN!

E: *sin!*

sin.

sin

. . .

(surprising)

. . .

(doesn't even sound like me any more)

. . .

GODDESS: *satisfied?* goes.
a goddess's grand going.

. . .

E: *defied?*

1:14 a.m. IM

oh don't ask

it's the
anonymity i guess, the
sense-less-ness of it
. . .

sense-
less-ness

remember michael jackson's
sense-deprivation tank?
(i almost typed self-deprivation)
. . .

?
. . .

u such a youngster

its a thing
u float in
artificial
environment
water at yr body temp, etc.—
hear 0, see
0
no sensory intrusions
. . .

alone with your heart
beat? not desirable
IMHO
. . .

no heartbeat even

it ws rest f/him
. . .

too much like Poe
. . .

to get in it

he ws *so* sensitive
just being n the world ws
2 much input
. . .

well it WAS self-deprivation then

like this you mean?
(messaging)
. . .

its what he did 2 relax
. . .

(sense-less)

= less input
. . .

well yes
(cant see hear touch taste thru
a screen)
. . .

you forgot smell

. . .

0 sense
intrusions at all

(god, this connection is slow)

smell 2

. . .

but its (this) not not-feeling,
not

. . .

knot knot knot!

. . .

deprivation,
exactly

. . .

no i know

Some time after that

her white hand
ceased to pass the poems
through the curtain

her low voice to sing
at the top of the
stair
. . .

remarkable, though odd
. . .

the verses

transgressed
the simplest rules
. . .

spasmodic

uncontrolled
. . .

and he didn't understand
why the curtain
. . .

A + Wiser Sympathy + wordless –
– silent – speechless –

How they are

always running ahead by themselves
is how

with like a wave, all melodic
catch you later

they want you to catch up
catch them
(or don't want)

they *never catch*
you

took her red silk off its hanger
& slid right into it
smoothed it against her body

(it flatters)

this'll show P
. . .

did an updo
put on Torch Scarlet lipgloss
wicked eyeliner

touch here

feel this

so soft

almost
like skin

E careens

through corridors

through the halls
of malls, mingles
in a high-ceiling restaurant's
crowd

                              (the laughing
                              could be a kind
                              of screaming)

. . .

says anything she wants
to all those voices
fleeing
the bodies that claim them

(and literally: bounces
off the wall)

effectively hidden everywhere

later,
outdoors:
        caverns,
trees, the overpass
canyon
alp

spends the day
everywhere (else)

. . .

the lake

. . .

Ars poetica

invisible to you, I

use a fountain pen   ink
blue-black
or emerald swirled with black

write in bed, wearing a long shirt

. . .

or write in pixels and ether
        write with light
durable words indelible

cross out, rewrite
write with a pencil
write   in sand
in water
in dust on the back of a truck

    Read me. Wash me. Believe me. Love

write in the midnight
it's a love letter it's a story

. . .

you can't picture

. . .

I write   four   drafts, you read one
write   forty

                               you read one

write weeping of a glad thing
can you pppicture

write in the dark, aslant, down the side of a page
you still never saw me

write angry so you can
           tell

just what you're waiting to read

I wrote a book and hid it

I wrote directions back

. . .

write   alone
always

just the way you read

. . .

we don't share the field
until I fill it

> ~~till it~~
> ~~fulfill it~~

my not seeing you doesn't keep me
from loving you, Reader

. . .

(yes, you)

Digital arrows

Eros pined

for P
(most beautiful)

spoiled boy

always got

. . .

miss/rulebreak
sashed & tiara'd
& pardoned & wed
            la la
            like that
as if it weren't
a miracle

were meant for her

stepping out of
mortality
as from a dropped
towel

. . .

& even he forgot
what she knew

& just stood there gawking

neck   breasts   waist
her unplumbable gaze

hypnotized him—all of us—
being there like that

. . .

E could watch hours
while the white dust from P's fingertips
fell as she idly filed

. . .

she was

a "looker"

her name by then
almost generic

psychic

       one who sees what can't
       be seen

the future
       secret thoughts
            what gods do

. . .

she doesn't need his
stinking lamp

. . .

It's futile—

Months, she thinks, *before*
either of those two
will try anything

. . .

Baby,
I'm trying to concentrate,

says E

playing with his new
technology

11:36 p.m. IM

eyewitness accounts
are notoriously
inaccurate

. . .

ur impossible!

. . .

just imagine

. . .

(or modest, maybe?)

. . .

unconventional
beauty

. . .

hmm
faith—

evidence of things not seen,
so they say

not sure im

. . .

yeah, modest, thats it

. . .

good at it

. . .

questions
test faith

. . .

u could be anybody
beguiling
an innocent (me)

(poor me!)

. . .

could be any body
cause im no body

. . .

i dont see the advantage

y not xchange pix?

. . .

isnt that
a fantasizers goal

interchangeable lovelies

many advantages!

. . .

this sounds like
rationalizing, not

. . .

mystery
adds interest,
for 1

(don't wanna,
basically)
. . .

fantasizing

& 4 2?
. . .

u cant judge this book
by its cover
. . .

ack

dont u wonder
about me sometimes?
. . .

o i think wondering
is wonderful

la la

Watches him

always at his lake
kneeling   studying

his bent flesh a wall

. . .

looking

(in Revery)
captivated

and tongue-tied

Rises and peers into
the water

troubles it plunging
his arm in

E in silence
and transparency

opens a hollow
inside

. . .

He stands and
whips his head around
looks back at the water

. . .

a goddess scolding
taunting

See?

Where'd you go?   go?
                                                     oh . . .

. . .

    this has to be
    the curse

        (it isn't)

The impersonal I

The Eyes attest

boast / breast / lost
test   Eyes test

. . .

Eyes violate and sunder
                    repair

The eyes (do) violate the Mind +
– the Soul

So the Eyes assault and plunder

. . .

attest
assault
convict and murder

nor He will to Boast

. . .

So the Eyes accost – and sunder

testimony render

. . .

Countenance of One

2:09 a.m. IM

enjoying life as
a nobody?
. . .

actually
we're both no bodies this way

(as in pixels & ether
. . .

"there's 2 of us u know"
. . .

& random
disconnects)

mais oui
. . .

"imagine unconventional beauty"
u said
. . .

mais oui
. . .

(may we? we
may)

(or may not)

if i meet u f2f some day
i won't even know it
. . .

f2f?

(french?)

. . .

dont u think thats weird

face to face
u know, in person
meeting in the flesh

(im afraid to use
my o so bad french w/u)

. . .

hard concept that

i was almost convinced
u were fictional

figment of a late-night screen

. . .

i am entirely nonfictional
(nonfigmental)
!!!!!!!

. . .

well, camouflaged then

. . .

this isn't hiding

i'm very open with u

which is y pix is a good idea
imho
. . .

multiple !!s are assaultive

u hide yourself otherways
. . .

incredulous!!!! that's all

for gods sake
. . .

anyway

looking at something directly
always
changes it

lets not

Encounter

Come out!   i'm out
                                                                    (out)

She parrots him,
flirty girl.

She hides, mouth full of his words
hovering
laughing

    —or is it a boy—
. . .

Who's following me?   me
                                                                   (e)

Essaying calm:

silence a goad
. . .

Who's at this lake?   slake
                                                      (ache)

Wind in cottonwoods,
the unsettling reverberation

it seems to be male, yes
seems to be
a young boy

repeating

—challenging?

What game is this?   aim at this
                                                        (amethyst)

Merciless.
Nothing.

Where?

Nothing.

Dear God!   god!
                                                        (god—)

. . .

Help! I am

besieged!   beseeched

                                                        (beseeched)

Mouth turned E-ward

(P close against Love's ear, kiss & whisper):

    Enough?

(never is)

    let's move indoors—
    let's have the lights off again.

    first time was so soft: hadn't guessed
    you were winged, downy as gosling,
    feathered, fuzzed—

                Love, what you hid!
                I took & took.

(kiss, whisper)

    dipped my face into shadow, didn't know
    who you were
    or what

Before that
there had been days when I thought
that by hiding my eyes, I was
invisible

ah Love!   & safe

it reminded me of then

(i was a child, it usually
didn't matter if anyone saw me)

i learned not-seeing
for camouflage

took & took

adagios of i-loves   what days they were!

(langourous stretch,
a tiny peck on Love's beardless
babysoft neck)

then wanted you to see
the real
me

so of course i peeked

so
much trouble—

i fudged an exit   married well
married my god you

(enough, you say?)

cover my eyes, E
don't look

pretend it's then

stroke me again
with your invisible
                    wide
                              wings

Dark bar

       This one loves me, I'm
       thinking

(O playing with her fingers in that place
that makes great margaritas)

(singing *I can't take my eyes off
your hair*
          literally, crooning it)

(loosening her barrette)

O, he sings all the time

(tracing his name with his fingernail
on her palm)

Eurydice's red hair is elemental
(singing)
it's fire   it's witchery

(leaning over to kiss her neck)

(running his thumb over her lips
until he's all Torch Scarlet)

O this one, I'm thinking,
won't leave me behind

like them

(looking into her eyes   deep
as if it were touching)

I'm thinking

(touching)

it's heaven

Disguised

Loved—oh, the springtime, as girls do
little birds   Mrs. Browning   flowers
    day lilies
    lilacs & heliotrope
& every letter a loveletter

her day thankfully bereft of explanation

    Pain – has an Element of Blank –

& every friend a love
a Daisy pressed into a greeting
all those Diminutives

carved in Alabaster

     wild rabbit. not shy—*hyperbolically* shy.
     virginal. powerless. minnowflash
     (madwoman?)   girlish

flittering
each a camouflage

E selfcaged—

soft frightened breathless childlike
he said

      volcanoes   thunderbolts
      kneading winds
      in her chamber meanwhile

      – the Billows tossed me up –
      no reins, all

      passion (all senses)—

that's why
the curtain

At the worst of it

the shoreline:

seagulls say anything

shriek

want want

I'm here

(here)

cries to the ocean
with almost her own words

want

(want)

waves
heaving   *(sigh)*

(I love the beach—)   *(sigh)*

(it's so relaxing)   *(sigh)*

Next time she looked

E had learned
the new tool's
language—

bent it to his
scheming
like his best old bow

the invisible target

                              aches

to be seen

How E had
sped up the process
with his ethereal connections!

Darling boy—

I fall farther for you
farther daily—

hours he plays at it

8:40 p.m. IM

strange day today

i was downtown for lunch
& a few tables over i was sure
i saw my ex

. . .

!

was it?

. . .

uncanny,
head held the same way,
same posture

i kept staring, trying not
2 look

then a gesture—i was sure—

but then not (a new angle,
someone got up)

then obviously

not

. . .

heh, good

. . .

(im ashamed to admit
i felt panicky
almost scared)
. . .

well who wouldn't if
u didn't
want to see them
. . .

i never used 2 feel like that

& even after
i kept sneaking looks, checking
even after i knew it wasnt
. . .

we all do that, i think

esp if its somebody we hope
it isnt

its funny
they move or something
. . .

never happened
to me before
. . .

& it starts all over again (is it? is it?)
. . .

im still kind of shaky!
. . .

here
let me hold you

there there
. . .

its so stupid

why should it even matter?
. . .

better now?
. . .

yes

im surprised but yes

Turns out he was famous

the liar player

. . .

Orpheus, he's been all over
the known world they said

Never saw the likes of you
he said

. . .

looking locking right into her eyes
as if they were feeding him

the lyre player

platinum, paparazzi, limos

The updo downdone & his fault
like her careful maquillage
coming off
        from kissing

& he whispered *that dress*

don't wear it again—save it
for just us

. . .

O
yes

Lake

can't you see it
from my point of view?

nothing

nobody

. . .

direct invite

come on, the swimming's good here!

or we could canoe

love you!
if you

could hear!
dear

anew
woo

why won't you even talk with me?   talk with me!
                                                           with me

. . .

suddenly

the boy
beneath him,
in the water all this time

looking at him

sound of the splash   *[a gasp]*

. . .

resurfacing
[choking, a kind of gulping]   *[a kind of sobbing]*

it goes on

. . .

then nothing   *[nothing]*

nothing

Dead air

You turn on your usual station
and nothing

                         : that sound.

Non
sonic.

Reader?

. . .

Hello? as if
calling down a hallway
for a door to open

                    : hello?
. . .

Zilch in the inbox.

You know this silence.

Cons/dole

Dear E –

. . .

         the Dooms of Balm

     (*consolari,* to comfort)

     (she being caught+ forever in that Wood
too quietly

     +kept

and lonely)

. . .

her caper part
hidden / unseen / subraidar

dearest E –

A Route of Evanescence

the *overtakelessness*

herself so Evanescent, to lose him to a bloom

    condolere, to feel another's pain

That awful stranger –
Consciousness

a wo

    your E

Gist

they have no bodies to each other
they have words

each has the words of the other's body

the dark between them the same dark
as between stars

& almost as much of it

12:02 a.m. IM

theres no such thing
as a virtual relationship

A.I., OK maybe, but
artificial emotions
no

if the bodys never involved
theres no point

is there?
. . .

. . .

. . .

Elected element

E took to living in E's house
(with her)

not such a small house, really—

the kind of friendship
where the space between you
doesn't fill with words

E comforts E—

both their loves didn't know
what the said things
meant

silence is
perfectest communication

neither cares to elaborate

. . .

both a little crumpled
from their time in the world

the curse—

> whatever she says, people
> turn into
> *what they expect to hear*

> are never correct

> plain as she says it

. . .

the upstairs room
crowds with empti
ness

. . .

welcome to woman, says E

XOXOX

You're a knockout, says O
and at the party
everyone stared

(*Isn't she a knockout?*)

and some guy goes
She's blushing

They don't know my name

it's ridicule

     Red's in white, ha
     ha ha

like P
or a bride
. . .

and women

his fans I guess

always around
gawking

     like men do

I thought you liked
to be noticed,

O said

I do—
I did I
thought I did

his crowd mobbed him
(wild girls)

      (concert screams)
. . .

when I stayed behind
he looked back at me
from his pack of fans

the last
I saw

of him

To the Reader

When you disappeared
the wall that stopped my words
            (*apprehend*)

dissolved.
Like light they sped out and away
looking for their mirror.

. . .

as always

you get to say when it's over.

Notes

p. 13: The phrase "girl with no door on her mouth" refers to Echo. See Anne Carson, "The Gender of Sound," in *Glass, Irony and God* (New York: New Directions, 1995), quoting Sophokles.

p. 20: The phrase "remarkable, though odd" is from Thomas Wentworth Higginson's response to a friend, speaking of Emily Dickinson's verse, as cited in the introduction to *The Complete Poems of Emily Dickinson*, ed. Thomas H. Johnson (Boston: Little, Brown and Company, 1960). The words "spasmodic" and "uncontrolled" are quoted by Dickinson in letter 265 to T. W. Higginson in Thomas H. Johnson, *The Letters of Emily Dickinson* (Cambridge, Mass.: Belknap Press of the Harvard University Press, 1986).

p. 20: The last two lines are a quotation from Dickinson's poem #780, in *The Poems of Emily Dickinson*, ed. R. W. Franklin, Variorum edition, 3 vols. (Cambridge, Mass.: Belknap Press of the Harvard University Press, 1998). Dickinson used pluses and minuses in her manuscripts to designate alternate/additional readings of her poems. Her early editors routinely, and apparently arbitrarily, chose from among these words (or sometimes substituted their own).

p. 38: "Revery" is Dickinson's preferred spelling, as in poem #1779 (Franklin).

p. 42: The lines "So the Eyes accost – and sunder" and "Countenance of One" are from Dickinson, poem #792 (Franklin).

p. 54: Italicized line is from Dickinson, poem #760 (Franklin).

p. 56: The phrase "soft frightened breathless childlike" is from letter 342a in Johnson, *The Letters of Emily Dickinson*. The letter is from Col. Thomas Wentworth Higginson to his wife, after meeting

Emily Dickinson in person. The phrase "the Billows tossed me up" is from Dickinson, poem #514 (Franklin).

p. 70: "overtakelessness" is from Dickinson, poem #894 (Franklin).

p. 71: Italicized lines are from Dickinson, poem #1325 (Franklin).

p. 75: "perfectest communication" is from Dickinson, poem #1694 (Franklin).

JANET HOLMES

is an award-winning poet who has published widely in journals and anthologies. Her poetry books include *Green Tuxedo* and *Humanophone,* also published by the University of Notre Dame Press.